The Voices Project 2015:
BETWEEN US

The Baby Elephant Walk by Joel Burrows
Mahla Land by Tahlee Fereday
Two by Two by Sharni McDermott
Say, 'Yes' by Tom Mesker
Sure by Julia Patey
Leo and the Ant by Callan Purcell
Petrol Station by Kathleen Quéré
Night Shift by Caitlin Richardson
Jun/John by Disapol Savetsila
Accidents Happen by Fiona Spitzkowsky
Pink Hair by Amanda Yeo

CURRENCY PRESS
SYDNEY

ATYP
Australian Theatre
for Young People

First published in 2015
by Currency Press Pty Ltd,
PO Box 2287, Strawberry Hills, NSW, 2012, Australia
enquiries@currency.com.au
www.currency.com.au

The Baby Elephant Walk © Joel Burrows, 2015; *Mahla Land* © Tahlee Fereday, 2015; *Two by Two* © Sharni McDermott, 2015; *Say, 'Yes'* © Tom Mesker, 2015; *Sure* © Julia Patey, 2015; *Leo and the Ant* © Callan Purcell, 2015; *Petrol Station* © Kathleen Quéré, 2015; *Night Shift* © Caitlin Richardson, 2015; *Jun/John* © Disapol Savetsila, 2015; *Accidents Happen* © Iona Spitzkowsky, 2015; *Pink Hair* © Amanda Yeo, 2015.

Cataloguing-in-publication data for this title is available from the National Library of Australia website: www.nla.gov.au

Typeset by Dean Nottle for Currency Press.
All photographs from ATYP's 2014 National Studio by Jennifer Medway.

Currency Press acknowledges the Traditional Owners of the Country on which we live and work. We pay our respects to all Aboriginal and Torres Strait Islander Elders, past and present.

Graeme Wood
f o u n d a t i o n
This publication was supported by the Graeme Wood Foundation

Contents

Between Us

Tom Mesker is an actor and writer from Sydney's Northern Beaches.

Throughout 2014 Tom was ATYP's writer in residence, writing short plays for workshops and a full length play. His role came after Tom was one of ATYP's 4x4 Fresh Ink writers in 2013 where under the mentorship of Jane Bodie he wrote *Strike, Strike, Snap* and *Homebase* which received staged readings, and *When it Rains it Pours* for the 24 hour Playwriting Project at the Griffin Theatre. In 2012 he attended the Fresh Ink National Studio and wrote 'The Mangroves', included in *The Voices Project 2013: Out of Place* production and publication.

Prior to this Tom studied Theatre and Media at CSU Bathurst, performing in and co-creating many theatre projects, and for his final work he wrote and directed *Portraits*, a site-specific theatre event. Since then he has attained a Certificate in Drama and Performing Arts, AMEB, wrote *Spinning* for Melbourne's Short+Sweet festival and has performed in multiple stage plays and short films. Tom has facilitated workshops in improvisation and also tutors drama to high school students, focusing on HSC performance development.

As an actor Tom most recently performed in *The Oligarch's Circuit* at the Old Fitz Theatre in 2013. He is now studying acting full time at NIDA.

Secrets: Introduction
Tom Mesker

I pick my nose. Like, all the time.

When I was ten my sister was being a big meanie so I rubbed her toothbrush in the toilet bowl.

I tell people that I almost went to a private school so I seem richer than I am.

I hate that instagram photo but I just, 'double tap', liked it.

I've been in love with you since I met you in November 2010. I've imagined our life together a gazillion times, in detail. I still totally think we'll get married.

I obsessively clean my ears.

I have in-depth conversations with myself. And reply.

I went to Alcoholics Anonymous for six months. I still don't know if I'm actually an alcoholic.

I two-timed my year four girlfriends.

I think I'm a great singer.

I tune out when you talk.

I told my mum that my school didn't issue attendance sheets anymore with our school reports. I actually just put it in the bin at the BP down the road.

I think I want my dad to die.

I went through your bedroom when you were away and borrowed your clothes.

I just said that was fine but it wasn't.

I was convinced when they were casting Harry Potter that they would somehow find me and cast me in the role. Because I was basically a Wizard.

These are all things that I have never told people. Secrets. My Secrets. Some of them big, some of them small. Some have never been uttered or written down, until now. Some people I have told. Other people I haven't. I'm not sure why I have told some people some of these secrets and not others. Or why I am sharing them now. Except for the sister/toothbrush thing. I get why I didn't tell her that. That is gross. (Lucy, if you are reading this—SURPRISE! And soz...) I also get it's a bit weird to admit that I secretly wanted to be a fictional character or even worse... Daniel Radcliffe. (Kidding Radcliffe, you're all right.)

What makes a secret a secret? Why do we keep them? What happens to the secret once it is revealed? Does it go away? Does the reason it existed in the first place simply vanish or get fixed? If I told someone that I obsessively clean my ears, will that make me stop.

Secrets are intrinsic in all of us. For whatever reasons we start keeping things to ourselves. Things that are only ours. Things we lock up. Things that we don't want to say in case they hurt someone, or embarrass us. Things that you've done that you feel ashamed about. Things that change the way people view you, the way you view yourself. Things that change EVERYTHING. Things that for one reason or another, if another person found out about, you could quite simply die (or change your name and skip countries). Secrets are potent and powerful.

So are this year's monologues that were written at ATYP's National Studio for the consistently brilliant Voices Project. When I heard that the subject of this year's monologues was going to be 'Secrets' I let out an audible and involuntary 'Ooooohhhhh!'. Like someone told me something REALLY juicy. Why did I react like I'd been told 'Sally totally pashed Jen's BF at the party on the weekend'? Because the dramatic potential is huge. I'd go so far as to say that secrets are vital to playwriting or writing a monologue. For example, subtext— what is this character hiding? What are they really trying to say? Or, the way an audience finds out information—does the scene or monologue slowly leak its secrets? Or do they all get revealed all at once? Characterisation—what are the characters' secrets? How has that made them who they are today? Relationships—Why are you telling this person? Why now? What is at risk if these secrets are revealed? Or the overall idea of the scene or play—What is it about?

Introduction

How can you conceal that? Scenes work well when they are about something bigger than what we see in front of us. When writing I think all these questions need to be asked. When I'm acting I love to pick up scripts that keep me second-guessing, it's the same when I'm an audience member, so it makes sense when I write to strive for that.

Secrets are such a great tool for creating dramatic structure but also opening up technique and delving into character and plot. Another not-so-secret secret to writing is putting yourself in your work. It's a well-known and well-rehearsed adage, 'Write what you know', but it is so true. Make it real. Make it personal. Put that little thing in it that can only be described as your 'you-ness'. How much or little of yourself you put in your work can be your secret.

This year's theme is vast, epic, incredibly personal and makes for some seriously beautiful and frightening monologues. I'm now going to let you in on a secret. All of those secrets I told you. They're not true. Well, not all of them. Some are and some aren't. Or alternatively... all are or all aren't. I'll let you decide. And I'll keep the rest a secret.

Tom Mesker is ATYP's inaugural Resident Playwright for 2014.

The 2014 Voices Project comprises monologues chosen from works written as part of ATYP's National Studio 2014. This is a week-long residency in which 20 of the finest emerging playwrights from around the country gather to develop their craft as playwrights and strengthen their playwriting networks. This year, they were guided under the mentorship of: Jane Bodie, Jane Fitzgerald and Ross Mueller. This project is made possible by the support of the Graeme Wood Foundation. For more information please visit: www.atyp.com.au/writing

National Studio Participant Emme Hoy composes her monologue by the Shoalhaven River

Ross Mueller leads a session on playwriting craft with the 2014 National Studio Participants 2014

Participants and mentors from the 2014 National Studio, Bundanon

Writing to a deadline at the 2014 National Studio, Bundanon

THE BABY ELEPHANT WALK

JOEL BURROWS

CALEB, a teenage boy, storms into his bedroom. He car-crashes his schoolbag onto the floor.

Fuck! Can they do anything right? The council is tearing it down, and it is absolute bullshit. They have got their giant cocking cranes and their small cunty dozers, and they're just tearing it all down. They're going to murder Fergus, the inflatable gorilla. They're ripping down the miniature Harbour Bridge and replacing it all with a laundromat. A fucking laundromat! I can literally, think of nothing more unpleasant. The only people having fun at laundromats are those old creepy dudes that offer to help out, just so they can touch your underwear. Is that what this council wants? To exchange family fun with cleaner pedophiles? Like seriously, what the fuck? What has happened to this town? I'm really sick of this council bullshit. I hate their show-pony ideas, and their stupid balding fat fucking faces, and I hate that when I talk about them, I sound exactly like my titty-littering bitch of a mum.

Beat. CALEB attempts to recompose himself.

And you know what is even more bullshit? Nobody gets that this is a big deal. Like yesterday, I get home from school, slam my lunch-box carcass onto the bench, and I just make a beeline straight towards the fridge. Me thinking that nobody's home to hear me take a bowl of cereal to my room, I project to my imaginary scribe:

CALEB changes his voice to become melodramatic, deeper and more like an upper-class gentleman.

'Dear Councilmen, In relation to your recent decision to demolish the minigolf center: it's a fucking travesty. Please consider another option or prepare to anal probe yourself. Sincerely, Caleb Anderson.'

CALEB reverts back to his normal voice.

But I wasn't the only one home. Dad, my dad, was in the lounge room. You know, home from work early. And he looks up at me through a haze of paperwork. And I just stop cold. I stand in our hallway; I wait for him to say something. Because I've been a pretty shit person this week, like more than usual. He knows it; I know it. I've been a massive dick to Mum, like actively avoiding her, talking, eye contact, you name it. I've been haunting pleasant evenings with one-word answers and half-assed shrugs. And every time he's asked me what is wrong, I've just said 'minigolf'. And he's just responded back like I was making a bad joke. So I just stand there, in the hallway, waiting for him to speak.

But he doesn't. He doesn't say a word. My dad just shakes his head. And then he gives me this really fucking queer look, like I'm not quite the child he ordered from the baby factory. It's a special cocktail halfway between disappointment and judgmental frustration. The combination of his tired eyes and his shaking bottom lip just punches me in the fucking gut. It was as if he has the power to make the whole room mutter, 'Caleb, just shut up. Minigolf isn't a big deal and that is no excuse for your behaviour. Could you at least try growing up?' Before he picked up his pen, and receded into the classroom inside his mind.

CALEB exhales or sighs.

Not a big deal. Not a big deal. Bullshit it's a not big deal! What is wrong with this town? We're losing mini! Golf! The last novelty sports centre in Wagga! Bowling is dead, laser tag is dead, rock climbing is dead. It's all fucking going, going, gone. And everyone is acting like this is not a big deal! Like we're not losing anything. Like I'm reacting like epilept Meg at Year Seven disco, or I'm high or something. That I'm the one being crazy.

But I'm not. I swear to fuck and back I'm not...

You know, you know what the minigolf is like? It's like a song from your childhood. Okay imagine: Your mum is driving you down Baylis Street, to your minimum shit wage job. And you're not talking, just staring out at the powerlines, so she turns on the radio. And your favorite childhood song is on. Without realising you start to nod. You smile. You tap the tune on top of the dashboard; you may even hum along. And then you say, very slowly, muttered under your breath, 'Man, I love this song'… But as soon as you utter that sentence, you're so fucking wrong.

Because it's a bad song. It's a really bad song. It is a very, a bad bad bad song, that deep down you don't even like. Honest to God shit. And you kind of know it. In the deepest socket of your soul, and in your milky bones. When you say, 'Man, I love this song', you're just cutting yourself off before you really think it through.

And what you feel underneath that sentence is completely different. What you're feeling is, 'Man, I really miss being seven. I miss how the shapes and colours felt different, and magic. How this street used to be twelve feet higher, with imaginary cars being parked everywhere. I miss Yu-Gi-Oh and fish fingers. I miss playing minigolf with my dad every Sunday and not… and not knowing that my mum was going to cheat on him in ten years. I miss how my mind worked before I walked in on Daniel, my hockey coach, fingering her, my mum, across the lounge room floor… and how then she sat me down, and said, and said that she loved me, and that I was a good kid, but I couldn't tell Dad, that I would not tell Dad, or it'll ruin everything. That this would be our thing that we have to keep hidden. I miss feeling safe in my own house. I miss being able to look at my mum to my right, in our car, and without me shaking. I miss when stuff wasn't a big deal, and I didn't have to grow up, because right now I'm trying to grow up, I'm trying really hard, and it isn't fucking working, because I don't know if it is more grown-up to break families or to be someone that I hate.'

Pause. CALEB lets his emotional leftovers shake out.

And that is what minigolf is. It's a thing you say when you mean something else. It's like a childhood song you think is great. But songs last forever; the minigolf is going away. It is getting torn out of the fucking ground. The council is ripping away the turf, deflating the creepy pedo clowns. They're smashing in the neon lights. They're exposing the skeleton and there is nothing left to hide behind. By the end of the day it's just going to be an empty lot. Tomorrow it'll be a laundromat. The council's leaving me with a laundromat, and a shit-ton of grown-up stuff I really don't want to think through. It's kind of bullshit, you know?

Fuck it, I'm telling Dad.

Beat.

I'll tell him tomorrow. Not tonight; Mum won't be home, she's out working late. No, she's not out working late, but that doesn't matter. 'Cause it'll just be Dad and me. We can have one more night of Chinese food, and football, and he can check my math homework. We can both wait up for Mum, for one more night. Yeah, I'll tell him tomorrow. It's going to be tomorrow.

MAHLA LAND

TAHLEE FEREDAY

MAHLA is sitting down on the grass at the oval.

I remember when I was five I begged my mum to drive me to Katherine for the NAIDOC Day march. We marched down the street with our bodies covered in steamers, tattoos and even balloons tied in people's hair. Black, red and yellow filled the town. I forced my uncle to carry me on his shoulders. I wanted to hold my flag as high as I could. I wanted everyone to see that I am proud. I am proud to have Indigenous blood in me. To have the blood of the traditional owners of this land permanently embedded inside me. I carry a piece of history with me wherever I go—like a fossil of this country. I wanted the entire town to see that flag and to see yeah, I am Aboriginal and I am proud. Well I… I guess I'm not Aboriginal. I was. Well, *actually* I never was. I was never Aboriginal. The Aboriginal blood, which I thought I had inside me, has been drained out and I don't know whose blood this is that fills my body! Whose blood is this?

I have just been thrown into the ocean with no anchor or lifejacket. Just me. Stranded. I'm just floating. There are no sweet sounds of birds singing. No horizon in view. No land or trees or anything that is filled with life. Just stillness. Emptiness. She just kicked me off that smooth sailing ship and abandoned me in the unknown, but *apparently* I'm welcome back on the boat at any time. Well who the fuck made her the captain of the ship?

I always knew that Tracey wasn't my real mum. But she fed me, sheltered and clothed me. Even though she isn't my mother I thought that culture was something we still shared together. It was sacred. Not something to be giving to just anyone who comes off the street.

Pause.

If I'm white maybe I should call myself something real classy like Alesssandra. I will move out of Barunga and to a big city full of white fellas. White fellas like myself. I'll do weird things like drink wine and eat cheese and say stuff like, 'How absolutely sublime' and 'Good job, old sport'.

[*Panic*] What if I'm not a white fella? What if I'm Jewish? Do I have to have one of those bar mitzvah things? Or African. In some tribes the females have to be circumcised. I hope we get painkillers for that. Or what if I'm Asian? I don't even like rice. I would be the worst Asian of all time.

I don't *have* to tell anyone. It's lasted this long and nobody knew. Did they know? Oh my God. Did people know? Am I the last person to find out? Are people talking about me behind my back saying, 'Look at Mahla doing the Welcome to Country and it's not even her country, she isn't even black'. Well obviously my family would have known. Would my extended family have known? But my extended family is like the *entire* community. Do these boys playing footy on the oval know? Do my friends know? Do I even want to know who knows? The town might go apeshit. I've been intruding into a culture that is not mine to witness. I have probably seen things that my eyes weren't meant to see and been involved in ceremonies that I wasn't meant to be a part of.

You know what? Fuck it. I'm just going to be a blank canvas. I don't need to know what I am to know who I am. To be honest I don't even care. I like not being anything. No-one can judge me for not accepting my culture and the ideas, customs and beliefs, because I got none.

Beat.

Or I can make my own culture! People ask me where I'm from I'll say… 'I'm Mahla-neze'… They'll say, 'Oh, where's that?' I'll just say 'It's… an island in the Pacific Ocean and it's really small so people don't really know about it'. I can have weird traditions like on Wednesdays we wear pink. Everyday people will pray to the God of Mahla before they eat, and they have to mention ten things they like about me in each prayer—like, how nice my hair is or something. And music. Music is crucial. I love Aboriginal music. The words and the beat.

I'll have heaps of rap music but without all that swearing crap. Songs about meaningful things. Real things. Like love and acceptance and family, not grinding bitches in clubs. And the dancing! The crazier the better. Heaps of crumping and just wacko free-spirited dancing. Without judgment. Without fear. And if you wake up in the morning and your muscles aren't sore then you didn't dance enough! Artwork will fill the streets. Everyone can be an artist regardless of talent. We all deserve to be involved in something beautiful, something that allows us to express ourselves. We won't need skin colour or blood to tie us together. We can all have matching friendship bracelets and that will be enough.

MAHLA picks up some dirt and starts playing with it in her hands.

It's like I'm at that Subway place, I'm creating my foot-long whilst picking and choosing what ingredients I want. What I think will satisfy me when I eat it.

What happens if I end up not liking the foot-long? What if I end up hating the ingredients and I find out I am allergic to pickles?

MAHLA starts to rub the dirt on her arms.

What if I'm sitting at Subway by myself and there is no-one to share my food with, no-one to talk to? What about if I miss my *other* food? The food that when I ate it, I felt fulfilled. The food that I loved to share with my family even if I was starving.

MAHLA starts to rub the dirt on her legs.

I wonder if Mahla Land will have sweet sounds of birds singing. Beautiful horizons as far as the eye can see. Land and trees filled with life. Aunty Peggy's rude jokes, footies to the face, hand-me-downs from decades ago, family meals, sneaky driving lesson on Sundays, no hot water in the morning, and that horrid smell of Mum's burnt damper.

MAHLA stands up with her body covered with dirt.

It does.

TWO BY TWO

SHARNI McDERMOTT

JESSICA, 17 years old. She is thoughtful, grounded, mature and curious. She has a dry sense of humour.

If I don't believe in God but I'm still a good person do you reckon I'll still go to heaven? I mean— if there is a heaven will God just know that I'm *kinda* good and let me in even if I've never believed?

I should have asked her.

Do you think you're better than me? Because of what you believe?

Maybe I will ask Amber. She'd tell me. Not like I give a fuck what she thinks. Not now.

You know when you meet someone and you just know they're a Christian. 'Cause they're *so* nice like almost too nice and it's a bit creepy but also kinda cool 'cause they just seem so positive and upbeat, to the point where it nearly makes you wanna die, but you also just kinda wish you were more like them?

You don't know, hey? Like you actually have no idea what I'm talking about.

But that's how I felt when I met Amber. She was soooo nice. It's like I instantly looked up to her. It sounds pretty wanky, and it totally is, but she made me wanna be better. She's just one of *'those'* people, like literally everyone loves her. She made me want to be one of those people too. I wanted in. I wasn't striving to be Mother Teresa or anything but I wanted to be a little less bitchy. A little less judgmental. Which actually made it pretty fuckin' hilarious when I realised that everyone was wrong about her. But it wasn't funny, not really.

I don't fully remember how we became friends. Suddenly I was just always at the house for sleepovers.

And I even started going to church with her which was… *weird*.

Hey—What's your favourite dinosaur? Diplodocus. That's mine.

You know that she tried to set me up with you? God that was so funny. Just 'cause I'm trying out this new be-nice-Christian thing does not mean I want my boyfriend to be a Christian. She was all like, *'He has a car and a full-time job and he even owns a house'*. And I'm like cool. That sounds gross and old and pretty fuckin' boring! I actually can't think of anything worse than having a boyfriend who has a car and a house and real job but he doesn't wanna fuck me…?

Am I a really bad person for thinking that? I am hey. But I don't think that now. Not anymore. You know that right?

Okay this is gonna sound dumb… but… what about the dinosaurs? Like where are they in the Bible? How do they fit into the whole scheme of things? 'Cause they are real, like we've all seen their bones…!

Do you ever think about why you're living?

Like what you're living for? Sometimes I think everyone else is living and I'm just existing. If I don't have a faith or a reason to believe that everything has a purpose then what am I even doing? I'm existing… floating. And it's pretty shit to feel empty like that. Alone.

What I really think is that one day I'm just gonna die and rot. It's that simple for me. But I probably should go to heaven 'cause I'm not *that* bad. Like I'm not perfect. I'm extremely judgmental and I really enjoy laughing at other people's misfortunes but I'm also not a pedo or a murderer.

How come when you're Christian it's a sin to have sex before you're married, but if you do happen to get knocked up then as soon as the kid's born it's like a real blessing and then nobody cares you're a slag?

It was really shit when I found out that she wasn't perfect. I wanted to be just like her and then I realised she was doing things that even I would NEVER do. Like ever. I can be an arsehole but I still have morals. Like I definitely have morals. Boundaries. Things I would—could never do.

Like she was always saying how her cousin grew up with a single mum and 'cause of that her cousin was a real freak. And she'd say all this stuff when she knew that *I* was the kid of a single-parent mum! And it's like… what? At least I'm judging you for something that you actually did. I can't help that my dad left. Bitch.

Beat.

Did you ever think you were better than me?

Even after I found out I kept covering for her for ages. Way too long. Eventually I just had to tell you. It's not easy to keep someone else's foul rotten lie trapped deep inside of you, especially when you've already got issues. I didn't want to hurt you. But I was also just sick of covering for someone who was treating us both like shit. Treating you like shit. You're too good for that. Way too good for that. Because you really are the best person. My favourite person.

And the diplodocus, it's got a really long neck and a super-long tail so it kinda balances it out. You know?

For ages I just couldn't tell anyone 'cause it was actually unbelievable! Literally nobody would believe that she was capable of that. And they especially wouldn't believe me if I tried to tell them about it. I'm a bit of a fuck-up and I've made a lot of bad decisions so why would anyone think that my word meant anything, especially against hers?

And then that night we're at her house and she asks you to drive me home, 'cause it's getting late. And I know what she's up to. And I'm thinking fuck off Amber you're not my mum.

But I just go along with it. I always went along with it. So you drop me home. I watch you drive off and then I go inside and have a shower. When I get out I've got this text message from her. *'Can you stall him at your place for a couple of hours for me?!?!'* And I realise she sent it ages ago. And I fuckin' freak out. 'Cause you've already left and you might nearly be there. And that makes me feel fuckin'—dirty is how it makes me feel. I feel gross 'cause I'm not ready to tell you but I have to 'cause you're about to find out anyway. You might already know.

So I call you. And you're still driving. I tell you to pull over. You do. And then I tell you, I just say it because I'm not really sure how else to do it. I just let it fall out. You know Amber? Well, she's fucking Ryan. Ryan Ryan. Like Ry from your church. Your friend Ryan. Ryan married-with-two-kids Ryan? Yeah, your Pastor. Pastor Ryan. Saint Amber, your sister. And Ryan.

And then I tell you that it's not just Ryan. It's Wayne and Pete and Roger and pretty much everyone, well not everyone but A LOT of people. Too many people. And that's not what you wanna know about your little sister.

You're silent.

Pause.

You're hurt. Really hurt. I hurt you badly in a way that I didn't think I would. And then there's all the other people who get hurt by what I did. Not what I did, what she did, but what I said. So many people are affected and I didn't really think about that part of the equation when I told you.

I never meant to hurt you or anyone else. I never meant to fuck it all up. But I did…

And. I'm sorry. For being annoying…

But… is it Noah's Ark? Is that where the dinosaurs are… or?

Fuck it's all so confusing. Now everything is shit. I mean everything, except us. It's weird that we are somehow completely fine but everybody else hates me. Everyone. I mean

I know they don't, not really. It's just easier to be angry at me I guess? Like blame me instead of all the people they really need to be mad at. It just *feels* like everyone hates me. But you don't.

And we're good. Really good. Which is so weird because I never thought there'd be an us. And now there isn't just an us but a really good us.

And I still don't believe. And I still don't know shit about the Bible.

But I know all the animals went into the Ark two by two… right? And maybe—I mean I dunno—but maybe Noah did that because he knew they weren't all perfect. And if one of them was really good and the other one was just kinda good or even pretty shit that together their percentage of good would just be enough?

I was wrong about her and I was wrong about you. But I'm glad that I was.

I guess I mean that because you love me and I love you. I am definitely better. Or… at least good enough.

Say, 'Yes'

TOM MESKER

LIV: Are you coming in?

JASE: Um.

LIV: Scaredy cat. You nervous? Don't worry, she won't know you were here.

JASE: Okay—

LIV: So this is it.

JASE: Nice place.

LIV: Yeah. It is. Mum's done pretty well for herself.

JASE: I'll say. And she just leaves it open?

LIV: Yeah.

JASE: But people could just break in?

LIV: I guess so. It's a nice neighbourhood so—you know, nothing like that really ever happens here.

JASE: Yeah.

LIV: Fuck I'm rude. Do you want a drink? Mum loves this stuff, Agrum, there's usually tonnes of bottles of the stuff.

JASE: What's that?

LIV: What?

JASE: Agrum?

LIV: Some Schweppes shit. Citrus blend. It's fucking weird but oddly delicious. When I first had it I was like 'Oh my god what's happening in my mouth!?' But it was okay.

JASE: I think I'm okay.

LIV: Water?

JASE: I'm okay.

LIV: God you're a pussy, it's just some water.

JASE: It's fine.

LIV: Do you want to watch some TV? There's Foxtel. I

sometimes just watch TV after school till Mum gets home. I watch 'Say Yes to the Dress'.

JASE: What's that?

LIV: It's some fucked American TV show where brides go to a shop and they try on all these marriage dresses. Wedding dresses. And they're like I want something glamorous, but simple, satin, chiffon, mermaid style with a train, with crystals, a veil, sweet heart neckline, because they want their day to be absolutely perfect when they get married to the man of their dreams and live happily ever after. They come out of the change room and cry and smile and the attendants are like— 'Does this mean you are saying yes to the dress?' and the girl, looking hideous, with all these trimmings and fluffy whiteness, snots down the front of her ridiculous gown, grins at her Mum and is like 'Yes, OH MY GOD! Yes!'

JASE: So you like the show…

LIV: It's fucked. But Mum records it. Like on IQ. Different tastes in TV shows that's for sure.

JASE: Will you get married?

LIV: You lolling?

JASE: Why not?

LIV: I just think it's crock.

JASE: Why?

LIV: What do you watch on TV?

JASE: MTV.

LIV: Yeah I like MTV.

JASE: Cool.

LIV: Do you watch TV with your Mum?

JASE: Sometimes.

LIV: What do you watch?

JASE: 'Location, Location, Location.'

LIV: Oh yeah I like that. I like it when they get a new house. Do you want to get married?

JASE: Of course.

LIV: Why?

JASE: I dunno.

LIV: Well that's not a good reason.

JASE: Well. I think it's a nice idea. Like if you love someone.

LIV: Do you love someone?

JASE: I dunno.

LIV: Okay.

JASE: But if I did. I'd want to spend my life with them. Make them happy. Know what they like. Like know them really well. Like if they said, 'I want two sugars in my coffee', I could be like, 'No! No, you don't you don't like sugar in coffee it makes you gag, you say it tastes like sweet curdled milk'. And I'd be right. See them change. Laugh at different times. Like when they're thirty and forty and how that's different to how they laughed before.

LIV: Are you funny?

JASE: Sometimes.

LIV: How?

JASE: I dunno.

LIV: You don't know much.

JASE: It was a dumb question.

LIV: You're dumb.

JASE: You're dumb.

LIV: You suck.

JASE: Shut up.

LIV: Make me.

JASE: Come here.

LIV: You know it doesn't work like that.

JASE: What?

LIV: Marriage. Life. Look at me.

JASE: You're alright.

LIV: Do you spend lots of time with your mum?

JASE: Yeah a bit.

LIV: What do you do with her?

JASE: Um—normal stuff.

LIV: Like what?

JASE: I dunno, normal.

LIV: Tell me.

JASE: Just normal stuff.

LIV: What is, 'normal stuff'? Tell me.

JASE: No.

LIV: Tell!

JASE: No!

LIV: Tell me what you do shit bag!

JASE: No!

LIV: I'll call the cops and say you broke in.

JASE: You wouldn't.

LIV: Wanna bet?

JASE: Do it. They'll take you too.

LIV: Tell me!

JASE: Um okay. But you can't tell anyone. Or laugh.

LIV: What? Do you, like, breastfeed?

JASE: Fuck off that's festy!

LIV: I saw this thing on telly of, like, adult babies.

JASE: Ew!

LIV: Well what?

JASE: Yoga.

LIV: What?

JASE: Yoga.

LIV: Oh my god what?

JASE: We fucken do yoga.

LIV: Oh my god!

JASE: If you tell anyone I'll kill you.

LIV: Omg that is so cute. When?

JASE: Saturdays.

LIV: Oh my god! Do you wear lycra?

JASE: No! I just. We go. I wear normal shorts and a singlet and we do a normal class, with her normal friends at a normal studio and it's very nice. Actually. It's nice. And it's normal. And we do yoga and it's nice. So. Yeah. I do yoga with my Mum. It's normal and it's nice and I quite enjoy it and I feel relaxed and zen after our normal sessions.

LIV: Show me.

JASE: What?

LIV: Show me your, 'Yoga Zen Master!'

JASE: Um—okay—you ready?

LIV: I am so ready.

JASE: This is Tadasana.

LIV: WHAT?

JASE: Tadasana.

LIV: What is that?!

JASE: They have weird names.

LIV: What?

JASE: The poses—Like 'Tadasana' and 'Baddah Konasana'. I never really remember them. I could be telling you the wrong thing. They basically just sound like jibberish. Annnnd moving into 'blahddybloopela'. Standing and breathing in 'I'm-a-loser-nasana'. Relaxing back into, 'look-like-a-bloody-dickhead-arunga'.

LIV: Look-at-me-I'm-a-wanker-nasana.

JASE: Bending into farting pose…

LIV: Don't-shit-your-pants-anasana.

JASE: Holding your arms in I'm-a-fucktard-arunga!

LIV: Feel the burn!

JASE: Feel the stretch! Move into I-like-you-anasana.

LIV: What?

JASE: Nothing.

LIV: Do you meditate too?

JASE: Yeah sometimes. Here… Close your eyes.

LIV: Okay. What do I do?

JASE: Nothing, that's the idea. You don't do anything or think of anything. Clear your mind. Tune stuff out. Like, me and anything else.

LIV: Okay.

JASE: What are you thinking about?

LIV: Poo-sanasana.

JASE: No what?

LIV: I dunno. Nothing. Everything.

JASE: Okay focus on your breathing and tune me out. Can you hear me?

LIV shakes her head.

JASE: Good. Concentrate on your breath. Let your thoughts come and go. As soon as they arrive let them go. Breathe. In and out. In and out. You sure you can't hear me?

LIV shakes her head.

Good. I um—I love your face. I love looking at you in maths. I know you look back. And I know I'm not the coolest or sportiest dude at school and I know that I do yoga with my mum. But I think you like me too. That's why I'm here, isn't it? That's why you bought me here. To share this with me. And I want you to know that that's cool. It's so cool. And it's weird. It's really weird. But I don't care. Because I like you and I want you to be happy. Like all the time. I mean I'll stay here and talk to her if you want. I will stay and introduce myself and talk to her. Let her know how you feel and that. I would do that. I'd sit on that couch and watch 'Say Yes to the Dress' with you. And her. If you want. Fuck. I kind of want you to say yes to the dress. For me. But that's a bit much, hey. We're bit a bit young for that, hey. Forget that bit. But you know. It could happen. I should probably start with just learning how you like your coffee, hey. That wasn't out loud wasn't it?

LIV shakes her head.

You didn't hear that did you?

LIV shakes her head.

You were meditating?

LIV: [*nodding*] Can I open my eyes?

JASE: Yep… I can do that though. Stay. Introduce. Me. You. If you want.

LIV: What's the time?

JASE: Almost six. When does she usually get home?

LIV: Six.

JASE: Should we go? Or I can go?

LIV: A little bit longer. I'll give you the tour.

JASE: Um—

LIV: Okay wait here I'll show you something.

LIV exits.

JASE: Moving into verbal-diahorrea-asana. Resting back in fuck-my-life-arunga.

LIV comes back with a photo frame.

LIV: That's me

JASE: Holy shit! Wow!

LIV: Yeah I'm tiny hey—she has it in her room.

JASE: Are there any other photos?

LIV: Nah just that.

JASE: You're her only kid?

LIV: I think so.

JASE: It's great she has this.

LIV: I know.

JASE: Do you want to stay?

LIV: Stay? Um. No. I don't think so. I like being here and I don't want to change that yet. I feel like—like if I told her she might not want me. Again. And then I couldn't come here knowing that. You know? Here, now… I get to pretend. I get to pretend for a bit. That this is home. That this is normal.

JASE: About as normal as my yoga.

LIV: Exactly.

JASE: When do you think you'll tell her you found her?

LIV: Dunno?

JASE: Do your parents know?

LIV: Nah. They say when I'm eighteen I can look. One more year. Don't know I found the letters. I can wait. I should wait. I should… put this back. Can you straighten up the rug? I like to leave it neat.

LIV exits to return the frame. JASE sees Liv's biological mum

arrive home.
JASE: Shit, shit, shit, shit, shit, shit!! Liv?! LIV!
LIV enters, still holding the frame.
LIV: What?
JASE: She's here. There's someone here. There's fuck. Fuck!
LIV: Go! Get out the back—out the back!
JASE: You coming?
LIV: Yes. No.
JASE: You coming?
LIV: Um.
JASE: You still got the frame. Liv, are you coming? Do you want me to stay? I'll stay. Here. Hold my hand.
JASE runs back and they stand still holding hands.
LIV: Um.
JASE: I'll go. You want me to go?
LIV: Um.
JASE: Are you going to stay?
LIV: Yes.
JASE: Okay. Shit.
LIV: Okay.
JASE: You're brave. You're really brave. Kiss me?
LIV: Yes.
They kiss.
Yes?
JASE: Yes. I'll be outside.
LIV: Okay.
JASE: You're great.
LIV: So are you.
JASE: What I said before—
LIV: Yes, I heard. And, yes. I like you.
JASE: Cool. Cool. Good luck.
LIV: Thanks .
JASE leaves and LIV stays. Frame in hand.

SURE

JULIA PATEY

SOPHIE, 17. She is warm, articulate but hurried in her speech.

Okay. I need to—
I need to tell you something
And I need you to just—not freak out. Okay?
I need you to listen. Seriously, listen. Until the end.

So I'm standing there at the wake,
At *Her* wake with all of her scummy family
That kid—that one with the nose ring?
He's there
So're the rest of them
They're just
They're picking through the cabanossi with the other kids.
The adults—her children—they're all clumped together
holding these massive glasses of wine
Nodding, sloshing, squeezing each other's shoulders and
saying things like,
Oh, Sue, it's so lovely to see you, pity about the circumstance.
Sue's nodding back.
I mean she's right.
It is a pity about the circumstance:
Kids are playing battleship with the cheese cubes
Older ones just sitting there on their iPhones,
Grown-ups waiting it out,
Before they start just chatting about random shit.

I'm at her wake and all I can hear is how much of a relief it is
that the soccer season's over.

And me
I'm standing at the cheese and crackers table
Just standing

Sure

Watching
On the out—
Right on the edge—
I find a glass with a bit of red left in the bottom
Look around
No-one cares
Down it in one
Tastes like shit
I can hear them—
Wasn't it such a shock?
find another dreg
Oh yes, well, she was still so young!
drink that
Before her time. Much before her time.
And then
A woman
She's walking towards me
Glasses on the end of her nose
and I realise Oh fuck
It's Anna's daughter.
I try to look away
Avoid eye contact
But I can't
Not in time
She spits
Spit right across the platters
Lipstick on her teeth.
You people aren't welcome here.
She means staff from the home.
You have to leave.
Wrinkles under her eyes
They're just like Anna's.
I'm standing at the table trying not to lose it
I've got my hand half in a cob loaf
I'm trying to get it out but I'm frozen to the spot
And I'm scared
I'm fucking SCARED
eyes filling, throat closing
that same lump swelling up and up.

And all I want to do

Is look across the room and find Anna—catch her eye—
so I look
and
She's there
Anna's there. At her own wake.
And yeah I'm fucken freaked out.
But I'm happy to see her
So

I raise my eyebrows
just to see
and she
she raises hers back
And then it's like normal
It's like normal and
we're saying
Are these people for real?
Just me and her.
Me and her.
The only two decent chicks at this thing.

We were—we were close. Closer than Nan and I ever were—I
don't know why.
We just got on. You know when you just get on?

The first time I met her—
I was at the home
I knocked on the door but she mustn't have heard me 'cause
when I walked in
Get out! Get out of my room!
She's hanging half out the window /fear in her eyes
Smoking. Like a cigarette. In a nursing home.
Even I know that's *not on.*
But she's just dangling there.
I dunno what to say—
Sorry I knocked but—
She cuts me off
And then you just barge right in?
She's looking at me
Right through me
Well. You're not gonna dob me in, are you?

34

No.
I say
Never.
I don't dob.
I got her a candle when I went on the pharmacy run that week.
'Kuta'. It's an island near Bali, Anna.
She'd never say but she liked that. Would always burn it on the weekends when I was there.
I wasn't sure, like, what she had—why she was there.
And she couldn't work out why I was there either.
Didn't matter how many times I told her.
She didn't mind.

The day she—
The day it happened
She's pretty crook
Nurses in and out all morning
Doctors too
It's not good.

Her family—they didn't come to say goodbye. Even when the doctors were saying that it wasn't looking too good. You come when it's not looking good you know?

So I stayed with her—
She was lying there
breathing rough
looking right through me.
The same way she always does. The same way she did at the funeral.
She looks at me and says
Sophie, love, you know I'm old.
And I say
Yeah, Anna, ya ancient, why don't y' just keel over already?
I was joking.
But she's looking right through me now.
No, Sophie, I haven't got long. I'm tired. I want to sleep but I can't, love,
I've been wanting to sleep for a long time now and I can't.

I understood. At least I thought I did.

She wasn't really living anymore.
Not really.
Not in her eyes
Not in her body
She was finished
She said she was finished
And it wasn't fair that she had to hang out until her body was
finished too.
The doctors had only given her a couple of days. That's what
she said.
We're talking about one or two potentially.
Two days.

I looked it up. On Wikipedia. It's illegal in Australia. Helping.
Of course it is. But what they call it. It—makes it sound as if—
Well, it wasn't like that. It wasn't. She wasn't helpless. She
asked me. Begged.
And two days isn't much in the scheme of things anyway. Not
really.
Not when you've already had so many of them.
That's what she said.

Two days isn't much Sophie
Not when you've had such a big life.

But what Anna's daughter said to me
About the staff
Not being welcome at the funeral
How I had to leave
It made me scared
It got me thinking that the family might know—that it wasn't
Natural. With Anna. Which sounded weird to me because she
was terminal.
They're upset—they're angry. Of course they are
But they must have been expecting it
They must have been told.

I went to the home this afternoon
Just listen. Listen
I just wanted to get some of her stuff before her family came
and got it all

Just the candle and that.

But when I got there.

SOPHIE takes a big, brave breath.

According to the home there's gonna be some kind of an investigation. Because apparently she was quite a healthy seventy-four-year-old. Not… not terminal as it turns out. Not two days away from death. Ready to die but not actually dying.

If they ever find out what happened— Even if there's a note. Even if there's. If it's with consent. It doesn't matter. Apparently you can't actually prove that that person wanted to do it. Not really.

And I need— She was alive and now she's not and I did that—I did that
And all I want to do is just find her and grab her and have her look right
through them and say— *It's what I wanted. Sophie did what I couldn't.*
But I can't. 'Cause she's gone. And now I'm not so sure.

LEO AND THE ANT

CALLAN PURCELL

LEO, an incredibly imaginative young man with scraped knees, a tender face and mud under the fingernails. He wears an un-ironed, grass-stained uniform and has a cheap backpack beside him.

I can see them…
Those shoulders cracking out of the flesh,
bones splintering the shell,
the thighs, the knuckles,
the meaty slabs hanging by the torso.
All blocking out the sun.
That keen sense of smell.
Then the bell.

A bell rings. He rips into gear and whips into his escape route. The following in a single breath:

Get t'ward the gate and cut through quite offen—
Too offen.
Keep pace,
keep going,
keep running,
stay running round the bend—
Shit!
A dead-end…
Psyche yourself and—
Slide down the drainpipe, that drainpipe muck
Aw yuck!
Stuck,
Aw *fffffffffffind the crevice,*
Ow! Yes.

LEO inhales sharply.

All dampness and darkness,

Leo and the Ant

*Cramped space to crawl through just feel the edge and brave
the ledge and
right along the timber board and breathe again—bright!
See right over the hill and another and another and—*

    His capturers nipping at the heels.

*Keep pace, keep going, keep running,
Keep pace, keep going, keep running,
Keep pace, keep going, keep running,
Stay running long enough till they lose the scent.
Drive straight into the reserve—
crossing soil and the shadows and stop.*

    *He comes to a halt. We hear his breath. He kneels with great
care, and lets the audience in on a secret.*

I love you. Not in love… all 50,000, 60,000 of them. Easy. A big,
fat, *family-size pocket*… A whole nest… like, like a huge pot of
coffee; blacky-brown… brewing… probably painful if you dunk
your dick in it… Not that I've done that… Not that I've dunked
my dick in a pot of ants. Not once. Queen Bee ant would not
be keen.

*Crack it back; the casing…
Sweaty,
Sweaty palms, sweat pits, sweaty forehead.*

    *He slowly sifts through the soil to find more ants; getting
closer to the core. He savours every discovery he makes.*

Like a year 5 volcano experiment gone wrong. It erupts in
a kind of foam, just wreaking havoc on every man and his
dog. *That* is what happens. Digging out this… this city with
underground routes, and roadways and stop signs… and
laneways lined with footpaths and pathways and parlours.
Imagine: lampposts either side; glowing—their flames
dancing in the bulbs—trailing off into the suburbs. [*Deeper
still into the colony*] And if you look close enough, in the
crevices are these homes with mailboxes… and pebble paths
and doormats and doorbells that chime.

He is amused by the thought.

To the right, you'll see the breadwinner heaving home his lump sum for the week, far heavier than he is, plonking it on the table. They dig in, under and all around it to their heart's content. And, and across the road on the second floor, the little one nuzzles into his mother as she hums and says, 'Good night, good night, don't let the bed bugs bite.' [*Pause*] In their hundreds of thousands, they still stand out from the crowd. Not like a fly, or a mozzie or a moth. I mean, a moth just sees anything bright and gravitates toward it 'Ooh this is nice.' ZAP 'Ooh this is nice.' ZAP... 'Ooh this is nice.' ZAP. [*Cracks himself up. Back to the ants.*] They've got routine. They know what they're doing. [*A thought.*] There's safety in numbers.

He finds an ant away from the nest.

Are you lost?

He grabs a nearby stick and fishes the ant from the ground. He never takes his eyes off it.

Slip under the edge... *the edge*—Yes!

Pause.

Stuck again... find the crevice—Aw yes!

Pause.

Along the timber... over the knuckle... and another and another and around... keep going!
... And onto the tip.

He and the ant exchange a look. He holds the stick toward the sky.

[*Laughs*] Look at you. Like a shiny, moving freckle...
You're on top of the world, little man.

Pause. He hears something from the shrubs.

Heart sinks in the ribcage...

Leo and the Ant

Too quiet—
Hold it in, hold on.
Tight chest, swollen lungs, goose pimples
—cheeky dimples won't win this round.

   He feels a vibration in the other direction.

Heart in the throat.
Fingertips, dry mouth. And eyes…
Fight or flight from the pack.
That sun is too, too bright.
Sweaty palms, sweaty pits, sweaty forehead.

   The noises advance on him, cracking the silence. He carefully
   places the ant in his pocket.

Stay there.

   Looking upward to the sky.

Shoulders cracking out of the flesh,
bones splintering the shell.
The thighs, the knuckles—

   He is punched, and then straightens up again.

Split lips and hands and open the casing.
Crack eyes and heart in two.
Peel back the crust and the flesh and the—

   He is hit elsewhere, struggling to stand. Pause. He looks his
   monsters directly in the eye and is hit once more, forcing him
   to double over in the dirt, and his mouth to fill with blood.

Bleeding.
Shit…
Hold it in, hold on. Don't bust.
Shit, shit, shit, shit! Shit! [*Into the open air.*] Scared pieces of
shit!

   Spitting the dirt and blood out of the mouth. Suddenly
   remembering the ant in the pocket he gets him out for air.

Well that was shit.

Pause. Leo and the ant become a gang. A wolf pack. He retrieves a bottle out of his backpack to clean himself up. For a moment, they soak up the silence in each other's company.

As a kid, I uh had a lot of things come after me… [*Ant doesn't understand.*] Monsters… [*Still nothing.*] I had a lot of nightmares. [*Bingo.*] A lot of bad, bad nightmares. Once, there were these eyes just looking at me at the end of my bed… Not moving, nothing. Just looking. And another time where I swung my feet over the edge of my bed, and two hands came up out of nowhere, just ripped me under it. Anything and everything you could think of, I thought of. If it ever got too dark, or too quiet, it would happen. You'd see it. You'd *feel* it. Then it was the fear of, these robbers—kidnappers, trying to get me and take me away. It all became more *real*, that whole thing… I dunno where it feels more real. But I couldn't get away, and I was trying to close the windows but they wouldn't budge, and I was trying to call out but no sound, nothing, no one could hear me, and that was, that was pretty scary.

But I remember I came home from school one day, and Mum, my mum, she gave me this bottle, this bottle, this… And she told me it was 'Monster Spray'. And she looked at me and said 'If we spray this in your room tonight, it'll protect you. It'll keep you safe.' I was so excited. [*Laughs.*] The night she sprayed it, I was on my back, stiff as a board, ready to go. And it was so hot you know, and sticky and sweaty, so I kicked the sheets off and the fan was creaking and Mum sprayed this mist… this magical mist… and it gently touched my arms, gently kissed my face, gently… covered the rest of my body. And for the first time in a long time, I felt safe. [*Pause.*] I need an 'Anti-Bully Spray', or a 'Fix It All Spray'… 'Get Your Arse Into Gear Spray'. No more stressing, sweating over… She was always clever like that.

Beat.

We used it for a couple of years. I don't use it now. I'm fine. Big boy.

I'm no bigger than you though.

This sparks an idea. He puts the ant back on the nest, grabs the bottle, and with the same compassion a mother would have when tucking in her child, he draws a circle of water around the nest.

Keep pace…
Keep going…
Keep running,
stay running long enough…

You're safe little man.

Fade to blackout.

PETROL STATION

KATHLEEN QUÉRÉ

OLIVIA sits in the passenger seat of a car. Waiting.

His car is brand new. Company car. Smells like leather. And chemicals. Sterilised.

The seat feels hot, sticky. Sweat drips down my back, makes my skirt stick to my thighs.

Seatbelt digs into my side. Rest my head against the windowpane.

Yawns.

I need to get out, walk around, stretch. I need a cigarette.

Beat.

He said he wouldn't be long. Said we just had to stop quickly to get petrol and stuff on the way home. He also made some joke about me having to get out and push the car. I laughed. But the joke really wasn't that funny. It doesn't make any sense. I couldn't push a car to save my life, 'cause I'm only like, fifty-five kilos.

I remember when I used to find his jokes really funny. I think it was his sense of humour that drew me to him at first. Emma would always cringe at the jokes her dad made but I would always laugh. It must've been that, 'cause it's not like he's outstandingly attractive. His blonde hair's thinning a bit and there are a few wrinkles around his eyes. I dunno. But he does look good in a suit. And he wears nice aftershave. Maybe that is considered outstandingly attractive for a forty-something-year-old.

Her thoughts are interrupted by the sound of her phone buzzing in her pocket. Olivia pulls out her phone.

It's Emma. She's sent me a Snapchat of her pulling a face and holding up the revision notes for our maths test. Caption says: 'I'm dying… help me… sad face'.

She looks at the picture on her phone for a moment and laughs. The phone buzzes again.

Still Emma. Text message: 'What are you doing. Question mark… Smiley face…'

She looks at the phone, considering her reply. The next part is spoken to the phone as if addressing Emma directly.

I'm in a car. *Your* dad's car, specifically. The same one he uses to drive us to netball games on Saturday. He picked me up from school even though he told you that he was working late and made you catch the bus.

She replies to the text message.

'At the library, studying. Sooo bored…sad face.'

[*To the audience*] Gotten so good at lying I almost can't tell the difference between the fake life and the real one anymore.

Beat.

I went with him to some cheap hotel, not for the first time. I knew it was cheap from the smell. Smelt like dust and dirty feet. The lady there gave me a weird look but didn't question anything. And the carpet was that horrible vomit-y colour. Why do hotels pick the worst colour carpets? I mean, really?

Beat.

Where the hell is he? Honestly, how long does it take to pay for some fucking petrol?

Beat.

This car. That's where it all started.

I mean well, sort of, not really.

We knew each other before, of course. Sometimes when I went round to Emma's house after school, or for a sleepover, he'd be there. We'd chat a bit. We'd have the most amazing conversations about stuff. Like actual stuff that mattered. Like politics and history. He always just knew so much. I thought he was so smart.

But yeah. Saturdays after netball was when it really began. At first he'd drive us both home from the games but then Emma got a gig umpiring for some junior teams that were on in the afternoons but he still offered to give me a lift home anyway. Which I thought was nice. He didn't have to.

Twenty minutes alone together in the car. Twenty-five sometimes if there was traffic. Or if we *said* there was traffic.

When he kissed me it was like the biggest fucking adrenalin rush ever. Heart thumping. Dizzy. Light-headed, like I needed an oxygen tank.

Pause.

Twenty-five minutes wasn't enough. So we started meeting up. Hotels. They were nice in the beginning, I think. None of that vomit-coloured carpet. I started skipping school. Making excuses. Told my parents I'd turned my phone off 'cause I was in the quiet room at the library studying. Started doing that so much my mum thought I was finally taking my life seriously.

Obviously my first time with him wasn't, like, the first time ever. I'd gone out with boys before. Normal boys. Boys from school. But I didn't like them very much. They all looked like overgrown twelve-year-olds. All bony with ridiculously long limbs, greasy hair, pimples and sweat. And then too much Lynx deodorant to try to cover up the smell of sweat.

Here was a man. A real man. And he was interested in me. And he smelt good. Felt sexy. Dangerous. But right. I didn't even give a shit about him being married. Didn't care about anything… except maybe…

Emma.

I think about her. What she would say if she knew. What she would do. Probably never speak to me again. I would probably never fucking speak to me again.

Beat.

Car seat's getting hotter. I heard once that you shouldn't leave like, little children or animals alone for too long in a car 'cause they might suffocate. I can see why now.

Beat.

Car pulls up next to me. Roll down the window and the smell of fresh petrol wafts in.

Shit. What if someone recognises me?

She sinks lower in her seat.

I really, really need a cigarette.

Beat.

Fucking finally. I can see him. Through the tinted doors of the 7-Eleven. He looks older. Sort of. If that's possible. Tired. Worn-out.

He's reached the front of the queue now. He talks to the man for a bit. Hands over a note, gets a few coins back. Tinted doors slide open, slide shut behind him.

He's got a small bag of groceries or whatever. He's taken this long and that's all he's got? One small fucking plastic bag of groceries.

Beat.

I can't do this anymore. I wanted to and now…

I don't know exactly when I stopped wanting to. All I know is that it was somewhere between our first kiss and when I started noticing the disgusting colour of the hotel carpets. Or how tired he looked. Or when I was secretly relieved that our netball team lost the semis so that it meant the season was finally over.

Her phone buzzes.

Emma again.

'Do you wanna come over? Question mark.'

I think I have to tell him.

Like now. Right now. In this car.

He starts walking over.

Here I go.

NIGHT SHIFT

CAITLIN RICHARDSON

SAM, an 18-year-old girl, wearing a soccer uniform and socks, stands on stage. A sports bag is on the floor beside her. There are three identically wrapped presents on the stage in front of her.

Sometimes when I'm getting ready for work, I put on my soccer uniform by accident. I don't know what happens—I've got my bag and I'm headed for the door and then suddenly I realise I'm wearing it.

Silence.

Suppose I miss it sometimes. The turf under lights. My boots. Kicking a ball against the wall till Stan tells me to piss off. The smell of the change rooms, pies from the canteen, Brooke and Matt and Dims and Nico and Joey and Sasha and Cal. All my mates. My family.

I miss running on the turf the most. But then when I'm driving home from work at five in the morning there's space around me and suddenly I feel like I'm there again. The world is flat and wide in the windscreen and for a few minutes, everything is clear. I know where I am. Where I was then.

SAM on her sixteenth birthday.

She goes to the first present and shakes it.

What is it what is it?

Hope it's edible. I'm starving. Wish I had—

She fumbles around in a sports bag and retrieves a piece of cake wrapped in Glad Wrap.

Crystal at work got this for me. I ate half of it before the lunch orders arrived. A piece fell into the deep-fryer. I fished it out but it burned my hand.

It still stings, but it's alright. Tasted terrible, but I'm alright. Had to try it.

She eats the cake.

Mum was going to make a cake tonight, but now she's got night shift. I'd hate to do night shift. I'd miss the sun, the light. It's getting dark now. Are you coming? For God's sake.

She opens the present. There's a Manchester United top inside.

How did you—how did you know I—?

This is too much.

It's… it's beautiful. It's beautiful.

Silence.

It's SAM's seventeenth birthday. She moves on to the next present.

What is it? Can I eat it?

I'm hungry, always hungry after training. Mum was going to make a cake tonight, but now she's got night shift. Marvin at work made me a cake though. Well, he lit a candle and wrote seventeen on a fishcake with tartare sauce. That's something I guess.

Don't tell me it's a Man United top again. That is way too generous and besides, I still wear the one from my sixteenth. It is a bit small now. 'Cause back then I was scrawny and my legs were too long for my body. I hardly ever turned up to training and I didn't buy the uniform in time and you thought I was a sook in my second game, but really I was crying because I had torn my hamstring and you had to carry me off the pitch. Ha! Got you that time, didn't I?

She opens the present. It's a Manchester United top.

Max! This is bloody outrageous.

I, I can't believe it. You are. The best coach ever.

Silence.

It's SAM's eighteenth birthday. She moves on to the third present.

Are you hungry? I'm so hungry! Should've bought snacks but there was nothing at home. Mum was going to make a cake, but now she's got night shift.

I just shook salt for an entire shift, but I was so busy I didn't even have time to eat one chip. It gets in your eyes, the salt. Chicken salt is the worst. I thought I was blinded once. Blinded by chicken salt.

I'll pretend to be surprised this time. I'll say, *'Thanks man'*, and punch you in the bicep, your sore bicep. I will.

But seriously, Max, as if I don't know what this is.

She picks up the present.

Feels a bit different. Must have loads of padding around it. Protecting it. Hope you, hope you haven't spent too much, like bought the limited edition top this time. Is it because eighteen is important?

You get better pay when you turn eighteen, so Mum's asking for more board now. I'll need another job. Something different, I'm tired of the deep-fried industry. There's a job going at the twenty-four-hour K-Mart. The pay is really good so Mum wants me to apply. It's night shift though, so I'd have to miss training. Won't have time for training. Yeah. Think I might leave this year.

Just kidding! You know I'm kidding. I just laugh at you because you're old and your knee is shot to pieces and you're basically bald now. Baldie. Do you like that? Or Basically Baldie, that could be your full name. Like that one?

Just kidding. You know I mean thanks.

For all those things, hell knows why you bother. Paying my rego and not telling the club. When Mum forgets to pick me up. Or that sports scholarship. Carol said she'd talk to the club about it—I knew it was you all along.

I know you think I'm ungrateful, but I do say thank you. I mean, I say things without words, you know. With presents. But not real presents 'cause you know how much I earn from work. But other things, like… playing well. I'm never late for training now. I'm the first one there 'cause I want to be a good player. Better than good. I want to be the best because it's the best and well, I love it. I really love it.

And you know I love…

She opens the present. It's a glittery red shift dress.

What?

SAM laughs.

Good one.

Silence.

[*Laughing*] It's a joke, isn't it.

Silence.

Must be. Can't be—

Silence.

I mean, where would I wear this? Like what were you—?

She looks at the tag.

It's… that's not my size.

Wouldn't fit.

It wouldn't fit me, Rob.

[*Shouting*] It fucking wouldn't fit me!

Silence. SAM folds the dress and puts it back in the paper.

I'm sorry.

Thank you.

She takes a K-Mart uniform out of the sports bag and puts it on.

People come to the customer service desk with birthday presents all the time. And they ask if they can get an exchange or a gift voucher or a refund even because they don't want it. But if they don't have the receipt then they can't. I'm sorry, but you just can't. It's company policy, why don't they get it.

If it's a present you don't get a choice. You can't take it back. You can't take that back. You get what you're given.

Silence.

Night shift's okay, you know. There's no traffic at 5:00 a.m. Just the road spread in front. The road running straight and clear and wide in the windscreen. Sometimes I get all the green lights and the world feels like it's mine. I drive without stopping.

JUN/JOHN

DISAPOL SAVETSILA

*Note: For a female performer, the name John can be changed to
Jane. The misheard name Jan can be changed to John.*

*JUN is sitting at a table, with a glass of water and a bowl
of mandarins before him. Three sticks of burning incense
are beside it, upright in a bowl of ashes. A babble of Thai
conversation from his family washes over him. It fades with
time, but never goes completely silent. JUN is fiddling with his
mobile.*

My phone's dead. Can I borrow yours? I just need it for a
minute. Dad?

He realises.

Oh. Oh, right!
What's the word? Tolah-tat? No, that's TV. *Tolahsahp?
Tolahsahp!* Can I have your… ah, *tolahsahp*… or is it supposed
to be *Tuh Muh? Muh Tuh?* Dad?

Please. Today's the state finals. They had Harry covering for
me, but he always sucked as Keeper. And he's got a bad knee.
I tripped him during practice, so it's kind of my fault, but it's
only a problem because you made me come here. Please. It's
six o'clock in Australia, so the game's over. I just want to know
whether we've made it through. I'll be back in time for the
next game, so I need to know.

Tolahsahp. Is that the word for mobile? How do I say 'want'?
Coe… Koh! Koh. Tol-ah-sahp. Koh Muh Tuh.

Tolahsahp! Someone give me a phone! I know you all have one!
Koh Tolah—

I'm not saying it right, am I?

Jun/John

Pause. The Thai conversation goes quieter. He takes the battery out of his mobile. Disassembles and reassembles as he talks.

I don't say my own name right either. At school they call me John. The name you gave me is so difficult for them to wrap their tongues around: Jun. Juh-AH-nuh. They stumble over the 'a' and it comes out as 'Jan'. John is easier for everyone. Especially me. No need to correct people, no need to hear them say, 'Oh, that's such an interesting name. What a nice language you have.' As if it's mine. I could throw two syllables together, say it's Thai, and people will trip over themselves to pat me on the back.

John's better. Cameron was the one to coin it. He misheard me when we met. I didn't correct him and it stuck. John. I wanted it to stick. That's why you never know when people call me on the home phone. They ask for John, and you tell them that there isn't any John in the house. First few times that happened, people said I was homeless. It was funny. Things got a lot easier when I got a mobile. I've made this thing last five years because it lets people call me John. No one needs to bother with Jun. I never once let this mobile die. The battery's never gone below seventy percent. But the power points here are different. I couldn't make the prongs fit.

I thought I'd be suited to this place. Like Darwin promised. Galapagos tortoises on Galapagos Islands. But Thailand is hot. The air is a stew of sweat and sewerage and petrol. As soon as we left the air-conditioned airport you took deep breaths. How can you like it? Even from thirty thousand feet I could see how bad it would be. The rivers, the roads, the blocky buildings are all muted, like someone's rubbed a skin of Vaseline over it all. It's grotty. Can't you see it?

He sees the bowl of mandarins in front of him.

I hate mandarins. The tangy smell when the skin peels from the flesh makes me want to throw up. Why did you put this in front of me?

He explodes.

I don't know these people! And they don't know me. When we stepped off the plane, they crowded me, crying, 'JUN! JUN! JUN!' as if he'd—I'd—never left Thailand. Fat uncles hugged me, aunties rammed their kisses into my cheek, and cousins swung off my arms. They did that and not one of them knows that I hate mandarins! Did you know?

Why did we even come here? Is it for Grandad? He died a year ago. So what are we doing here now?

We've lighted incense for him, and laid out dishes of technicolour fruit, and slices of duck, and chicken, and pork. What is that? Is that what praying is to you? You made me kneel and copy you, gesture by gesture and syllable by syllable. What were you saying? What were you making me say? I heard Jun over and over again. Were you praying that I'll do well in my exams? Or that I'll learn to speak Thai? Were you praying that I'll suddenly get along with these strangers? What are you saying about me? Are you praying that I'll just snap to and understand? When none of it makes any sense!

He grabs the incense.

What is this? Explain to me, please. Why does it have to be three sticks? Why do we have to put food in front of Grandfather's picture? Do you really think he eats it? You'd think a country with so many beggars on the streets would know waste when they see it. Is there a God that you pray to? Or is all just a bunch of dead family members like in Mulan? Is that what's going to happen to me when I die? A family reunion that never ends?

Do you think he cares about me? If I kneel down, put my hands together—

He does. Knees and balls of his feet on the ground, palms pressed together across his chest.

—and start praying:

'Grandad! Help me get it! Let me understand what everyone is saying! Let me speak!'

Jun/John

He waits for a response.

Nothing. He doesn't understand what I'm saying. How could he? He's waiting for Jun to talk.

You don't understand me either. How have you gone all these years without saying anything to me? Didn't you ever ask how my day was? Or what I wanted to do after I graduate? Why didn't you make me realise that I was forgetting how to talk? I'm walking around my mother country with the stock phrases I find in tourist pamphlets! *Sawadee! Kop Kun!* That's what you've turned Jun into. A tourist in his own country.

Kneeling like this hurts. After a few minutes, my knees are crushed, and the blood congests in my shins. It's like half of my body has died. You can stay like this for hours though. How do you do it?

Dad. *Tolahsahp.* Please, I just want to speak to Cameron for a bit. Nothing important. I don't care about the game. Just a 'Hello'. That would be enough. You don't understand what it's like to go days surrounded by babble. I found a grainy channel of *Home and Away* yesterday and I binged it until my eyes went red. I wasn't really listening. Just letting the familiar sounds wash over me. You don't know what it's like to be stuck in a place without being able to talk to anyone. In Australia you had Mum. You have me.

No. You had Jun. You used to laugh together when you talked about people right in front of their faces. Remember that PTA night, when he told you his teacher's head looked like a half peeled potato. You nearly choked trying not to laugh at him. It was like a secret language, all to yourselves.

But it was too much work. Secret languages are for kids. It atrophied like an unused organ. John doesn't need it. He's the type of person you talk about. Out of the loop.

None of you have understood a word I've said, have you?

He recomposes with a smile and a laugh.

Besides, you'll make some excuse about it to them. You don't want me to make a scene and embarrass you in front of your family. You'll say I've been toasting Thailand, or Grandpa.

I'll help. Tie this off as if I've been making one big speech. With a smile on my face and everything. I'll raise my glass, because that's something that everyone does, here and back home. You're smiling back. Are you really buying this? Or are you just giving up? I can't blame you. Here's to Jun.

He drinks. The sound of chatter grows. He goes back to his phone and tries to make it work.

ACCIDENTS HAPPEN

FIONA SPITZKOWSKY

VIOLET is in a waiting room at the ER. The pinkie finger on her right hand is badly crushed, she is waiting to be admitted. She is shaky, jittery, in shock, for one reason or another. She speaks to another patient.

Pretty gruesome, hey?

Pause.

They'll probably see you before me, though. I mean this was just a little accident and that… that is… oozing.

Pause.

I was just practising and I was really tired, and my left hand went to close the lid but my right hand was still playing. Pretty stupid, hey? Just a stupid accident.

Pause.

They say it takes ten thousand hours to master something. At an hour a day that's twenty seven years. I'm pretty impatient though, so I'm doing two hours a day. Nana's even worse: she wants me to do three. Four on weekends since I've got an audition coming up. It's a big one, for the conservatorium. On the twenty-first of next month. Usually I'm terrible with dates. I've missed so many recitals 'cause I got the dates wrong. One or two you could probably understand but I've missed—

Anyway, I can't miss this one because Nana reminds me about it every twenty minutes, just in case I've forgotten. She's circled it on her calendar with the boldest, brightest shade of red you could imagine. It wouldn't surprise me if she ordered it especially.

Pause.

She's going to be so mad. No, not mad, just disappointed.

Pause.

I think it will be alright though, I can pretty much stretch it all the way out and that's a good sign, right?

She tries to pull her finger out to its full extension, but can't. She keeps trying even though it is clearly very painful.

When I was growing up, Nana used to do this—stretch out my fingers—to make them grow longer. She'd stretch out each finger and nod proudly. This one will be my star pupil. This one will be my star.

Everyone says I've got her fingers.

But when we play duets, sitting next to each other on the stool, she's always just that little bit faster than I am, she hits the keys with more precision. Her fingers know where to go. But everyone tells me I have her fingers. So I figure mine will know too, I just have to practise. It's all about muscle memory. I mean, people talk about natural talent but—

Well, Nana used to always lecture me about how Mozart wrote his first melody at the age of three, teasing me that I've already passed my prime. It freaked me out, I wanted to quit and do something else, something without child prodigies so I could be the child prodigy, so other Nanas could tell their grandkids stories about me, but everything already has its prodigy. There's nothing left for me.

Silence.

[*Gesturing towards another patient*] I can't believe they're seeing him first. What do you think? Concussion at footy practice?

Pause.

If you practise hard enough, nothing else matters, right? It doesn't matter if your dad is a plumber and your mum doesn't have a musical bone in her body and your fingers are too short, if you practise you'll get there eventually.

Not that mine are too short, mine are long, like Nana's. Everyone says I have Nana's fingers.

And I practice heaps: repeating stuff over and over again. And not even the fun stuff. Just the basics. Scales. C major is a really hard scale, you know. On paper it looks like it's the easiest; no sharps no flats. It's easy to remember but physically it's tough, it's unnatural. The keys are too static, too close together, too similar for fingers of varying length, so to hit each key exactly the same—the same speed, the same precision—it's almost impossible. I can't do it, my fingers don't fit the keys right, I always hit the F too hard. My knuckles are too loose, apparently, they need to be bent, not collapsed. Curve your fingers, curve your fingers, girl I'm not really sure what that means, to be honest; I just wiggle my fingers a bit until Nana seems satisfied.

But I've seen Nana do it. The perfect C major.

So today was going to be my C Major day. C Major over and over again. And over and over again. And over again.

C D E **F** G A B C B A G **F** E D C. Not good enough.

C D E **F** G A B C B A G **F** E D C. Not good enough.

C D E **F** G A B C B A G **F** E D C. Can you hear that? The F? Not good enough.

C D E **F** G A B C B A G **F** E D C.

She finds her fingers following along, muscle memory, but twinges her crushed finger.

Shit.

Two hours. Two hours of C Major. Not good enough. Not good enough. More than enough for Mum, but she doesn't have a musical bone in her body.

She drags me away from the piano and gives me this big tough love speech.

It doesn't have to be perfect.

But Nana did it.

Nana has been doing it a long time. And she's got longer fingers than you, more nimble.

But I have her fingers.

No you don't.

Everyone says I have her fingers.

Yes, everyone says that, because they don't— Look, it's just an expression.

I have her fingers.

You don't.

I do.

Pause.

[*Slowly*] And she sighed. And she told me… She told me this with a straight face. I have my grandmother's fingers, but not Nana's. Nana is short for Nancy. The name of the woman my grandfather married after he found his first wife hanging from the rafters in their garage, not dead, not yet, because she didn't tie the knot right or something, but she died on the way to hospital, just sort of gave up again.

Silence.

Mum told me that with a straight face. She was only three at the time, she doesn't remember her mother. But a straight face? That's weird, right? You'd think she'd be upset. Or mad. Or disappointed. But no: totally straight face. That's worse, that's… nothing.

Pause.

A straight face. A strange face, I realised, that looks nothing like Nana's.

Pause.

So I don't have Nana's fingers. But everyone says I do. Which is all that matters, right? It's what's inside that counts? But not inside as in genes but inside as in determination or whatever.

[*Getting faster*] I go back to that piano, determined.

C Major C D E **F** G A B C B A G **F** E D C.

My left hand is good, fast, precise, but my right doesn't know where to go. It keeps nicking the black keys.

C C-sharp E **F** G A B C B G-sharp G **F** E-flat D B

And Mum's looking at me with her stranger's face, and I'm playing these scales with my stranger's hands and—

Long pause.

It was an accident.

Long pause.

It will be fine for my audition. I'll get better. If I really want to, I'll get better.

Pause.

If I really want to.

Pause.

I'm going to have to work twice as hard. Four hours every day. Five! And I'll have to do therapy and everything, I mean physio. Physiotherapy for my finger. I'll write the appointments in my calendar, and I'll go… I will go…

If I work hard, I'll be fine.

Pause.

I'll be fine.

Pause.

I'm lucky it was just my pinkie.

Long pause.

But accidents happen all the time. I mean, look around. I could get a concussion. Or get all… oozy. Or get a nail though my hand. Or jam it in a car door—*get it* jammed in a car door.

Pause.

[*Looking at her hand*] Maybe it just won't work. Maybe I'll work really hard but it won't be enough. I won't be able to hit the F quite right. Maybe I shouldn't bother with the audition. C Major is a required piece. Why waste their time? Right? I'm not giving up, I'm being realistic.

Pause.

And long fingers are good for other things too. Like…

Long pause.

… tying knots.

PINK HAIR

AMANDA YEO

ASH sits in a hairdresser's chair, shifting about as much as one can while at the hairdresser's. The hairdresser squirts her hair with a water bottle and combs it through.

I want to do something really outrageous. Like, my hair has always been around this length and I want something new. I'd like to dye it if the school would let me, but you know, uniform rules and all that. What I really want to do as soon as I get out of school—as soon as I graduate—is dye it all pink.

Mum says I should never, never bleach my hair because it'll just ruin it all. 'Cause she had this horrific experience when she was like, twenty. But hair technology has come a long way since then. It's been what, fifty years? So I reckon you could probably do it. I trust you.

I've felt badly bleached hair before though and it's all super dry and brittle like uncooked mee hoon and it just feels disgusting. It only happens if you bleach it too much though. So I only want to do it once, just to see how it suits me.

I guess I'll just get a trim.

The hairdresser begins cutting.

I just really, really want pink hair. See, it's kind of a joke, okay, it's a joke of mine. Well, not mine— me and my boyfriend. My boyfriend Dan, who drove me here, by the way, because boyfriends, that's what boyfriends do, they drive you places. Well, if they're good. Mara's boyfriend won't drive her anywhere but that's 'cause he's a loser. Anyway. What was I saying? Oh yeah, I want to dye my hair pink because me and Dan, we have this kind of running joke. See, I have no idea what he looks like. Well, I have some idea— I've felt him before. Well I— you don't need to know that. What you need to know is that ever since I've known him, whenever I ask what colour his hair is or what colour his eyes are he'll say something like 'green with red spots' or 'it's got like a pineapple pattern across the top of my head like a tiara'. 'Cause he's a moron. And he's managed to get everyone we know in on it and they think it's hilarious. It is, but... Anyway. So I want to dye my hair pink. 'Cause in my mind he has green hair. So now I'll have—do you get the joke? Yeah, anyway.

It feels like you're going too short. I told everyone I was gonna come here, so if I look like a hay bale they'll know it was you.

Pause.

Do you think I could get a wig? Not like a pink wig, that would be half-arsing it I reckon. I mean get a wig the colour of my hair and dye my hair pink and then put the wig on top of it for school. I know it's a lot of work and kind of not practical, but I reckon I could do it.

Pause.

We've been going out for—how long have we been going out now... like a year. And I have no idea what colour hair he has. And I remember colours—I fully remember colours. When I was... I think I was like seven, I could still see pretty well then, I remember going to the park with my brothers and it had been kind of rainy so it was really muddy and I slipped and I fell into this puddle of what I thought was mud—turned out it was dog shit. Then I threw up. But that's what I remember when people say 'brown'.

It's not so much that I care what his hair looks like. Hair colour means nothing, really, I mean, Jensen Ackles has brown hair but so does Steve Buscemi. It doesn't really tell you much so it's not like it's a big deal, you know. But like, not knowing is an inequality.

Pause.

Can I smell the shampoos later? I want my hair to smell nice. I don't mean like nice in general nice, but nice like have a

66

distinct—vanilla. Are there any shampoos that smell like vanilla? I know there are perfumes but I don't know about shampoo.

Pause.

I know he's white 'cause he loves quinoa and checks ambiance ratings on Eatability. His hair is like medium length—like twice the length of a really good shag carpet, and it's pretty thick. Not as soft though. Kind of coarse. And his nose is weirdly small. Like, it's good he doesn't have a giant beak, but it's like a nipple. He wears glasses sometimes and I don't know how they stay on. Maybe he has massive ears. The glasses might just be for looks—the lenses are pretty thin. But it seems like all he wears is print t-shirts and I don't know what's on them.

I like the way he sounds. He doesn't have an accent, which sucks, but he rounds out all his vowels. And he says 'dahnce' and 'plahnt'. Sometimes he does a Southern accent, but that's not really sexy and his French one makes him sound like Jabba the Hutt.

That still feels too short. Longer. Longer. Longer. Yeah, I said I want something outrageous but I don't want to look like a toilet brush.

He must have massive ears. How else would his glasses stay on? And they're proper big frames. Big frames are in now. He has nice arms—broad shoulders, mostly muscle. I haven't felt up his legs though. Like, they're hairy but I've never run my hands up them. What if he has skinny legs? You hear about those guys who are shaped like funnels. What if he's like a pipe-cleaner with a GI Joe torso? A GI Joe torso, pipe-cleaner legs, and a giant pair of fake glasses hanging off dinner-plate ears and a tiny nipple.

Pause.

But if he did look like that someone would tell me. They wouldn't just say, 'Oh nah yeah he has green hair', they'd tell me. Because it wouldn't look right. It would be like exploitation. It's taking advantage. And you gotta believe people are better than that—you gotta believe that if they see some guy, some like Swiss cheese faced soft serve cone guy taking advantage, they'd say something.

Pause.

I can get a pretty good idea of how hot a person is by how people react to them. If they're ugly people usually avoid them or talk to them with this undertone of pity. I get the same sort of thing.

Pause.

I'm a pretty good person really, like, I'm really smart and I'm on the debating team. I let Mr Lawson take photos with me for that newspaper article about special needs in schools even though like all of the teachers still forget to describe diagrams. That's all that should matter, whether you're smart—and I'm smart—and whether you're a good person. And I'm a good person. I'm on the debating team—did I say that?

I'm a good person so it doesn't really matter what my hair looks like. It doesn't matter at all.

Pause.

My mum tells me I'm beautiful all the time. So does Dan. So does everyone, really.

But if I'm not… If I'm not, then who would tell me? Would they tell me? Or would everyone just…?

Long pause.

I know I have brown hair.

Pause. The hairdresser finishes up. ASH sniffs the air and immediately brightens.

Is that vanilla shampoo? Can I get a bottle? That's awesome. Vanilla's gonna be my signature scent. We done?

Pink Hair

She gets up from the chair.

Next time I'm totally bleaching my hair. I don't really remember my skin tone, but reckon I could rock pink.

She tosses her hair, presents herself.

So. How do I look?

AUTHOR BIOGRAPHIES

Joel Burrows (*The Baby Elephant Walk*) is a playwright, director, creative producer and founder of Wollongong-based Theatre Versus Everything Productions. He has a deep love of the theatre, and a burning desire to tell stories about his upbringing in rural Australia, or his surreal nightmares about a sentient vacuum cleaner that attempts to seduce him.

Joel made his professional playwriting debut in 2013 with *The Boat, The Message, and the Fridge Full of Turnips*, which was presented in the Board of Studies' *OnSTAGE/OnSCREEN* and then performed by request at UTAS Student Directed Festival. He went on later the same year to co-write and independently produce *Theatre Versus Everything*.

He is currently in his second year of a Bachelor of Creative Writing at the University of Wollongong. This year Joel's work *The Cod Fish* was performed as a part of The Drama Studio's Final Draft Project. He is presently developing a new theatrical work *Pulp Theatre: Double Feature*, which will be performed mid-October at the Phoenix Theatre, Wollongong.

Tahlee Fereday (*Mahla Land*) is a young emerging actor and comedian in the Northern Territory. Tahlee's writing experience includes texting her friends, writing entertaining Facebook statuses and scripting and producing her own breakfast show *The Breakfast Show with Tahlee* on Darwin's local radio station Larrakia Radio.

Sharni McDermott (*Two by Two*) is an actor, singer and dancer with an Advanced Diploma of Performing Arts (Acting) ACPA. Her credits include *Parramatta Girls* (2014), *The Maids* (2011), *Stolen* (2011), *The Rock* (2010), *Soul Music* (2010), *Miracles in Brisbane* (2009) and *Equus* (2006). For ACPA Sharni performed lead roles in several productions directed by Leah Purcell including: *Low* (2010), *X-Stacy* (2009), *Q150 and Long Before* (2009), *A Midsummer Night's Dreamtime* (2008) and *Reflections* (2008). Sharni sang the National Anthem for the opening of the 2011 Indigenous All Stars football match, as well as being a lead singer at the National NAIDOC Ball and The Opening Ceremony of the Brisbane Festival in 2009. She has performed as a singer at both The Deadly Awards and the Brisbane Festival in 2008.

Sharni has also travelled extensively throughout Indigenous communities in Cape York in Queensland and the Northern Territory, working for both AFL and the Music Outback Foundation to facilitate theatre and performance workshops with young people. She has also worked with ATYP on their Djurali Program.

Julia Patey (*Sure*) is an emerging theatre-maker, writer and director from Sydney. Her theatre-making credits include *The Hand of Time* (Not Suitable for Drinking), *Where There's Smoke* (99seats Theatre & The Blue Room Theatre Summer Nights), and *Stockholm* (CSU/BATS). Julia is founding artistic director of Sydney-based theatre collective, 99seats Theatre and is a 2013 recipient of The Blair Milan Scholarship Prize. She holds a Bachelor of Communication (Theatre/Media) from Charles Sturt University, Bathurst and is currently undertaking post-graduate studies in Creative Writing at UTS.

Callan Purcell (*Leo and the Ant*) is a Newcastle-based artist. He has collaborated with companies throughout the Hunter region as performer, director, devisor and designer. As a devisor and performer he has been involved in CONDA award-winning *The Past is a Foreign Country* (Paper Cut Collective), *Fractured* (The Senior Ensemble) and *Diving Off the Edge of the World* (Tantrum Youth Arts). As an actor, Callan's recent credits include *Spring Awakening*, *The Twits!*, (StoddArt Productions) *The Complete Works of William Shakespeare [Abridged]* (Popular Theatre Company), *Romeo and Juliet* (Upstage Theatre), *Next to Normal* (Newcastle Theatre Company) and David Williamson's *The Removalists* (Stooged Theatre).

He made his directing debut with *Lord of the Flies* at Hunter School of the Performing Arts in collaboration with the Boys In Performing Arts initiative, and earlier this year led the creative team of *Aftershocks* to commemorate the 25th anniversary of the Newcastle earthquake. Callan was the resident lighting designer for DAPA theatre and has also recently designed *Death Trap*, *Pride & Prejudice*, *Wait Until Dark*, *Cat on a Hot Tin Roof*, *They're Playing Our Song* and *The Full Monty: The Musical*. He was the recipient of the State Shakespeare Award after writing and performing his adaptation of the play-within-a-play from

A Midsummer Night's Dream. He received the award Best Juvenile Performance for his work in *Beauty and the Beast* in 2011, and in 2012 he performed his group theatre piece at *OnSTAGE*.

Kathleen Quéré (*Petrol Station*) is a young writer/actor from Sydney. She developed a strong passion for theatre at a young age by becoming involved in countless school productions and writing scripts for her drama class to perform. In 2011 Kathleen's short play *The Bird* was selected as a finalist in the Fast+Fresh Theatre competition. Since then, she has been an ATYP Atypical Advisor (2011 onwards), a Griffin Theatre Company Ambassador (2012) and has performed in a production of *The Grandfathers* as part of the NIDA open program. Kathleen plans to study theatre and/or creative writing at university in 2015.

Caitlin Richardson (*Night Shift*) lives in Hobart and enjoys writing prose, poetry and scripts. This year, she has been a participant in Blue Cow Theatre Company's Cowshed playwriting program and an assistant director for the Tasmanian Theatre Company's production of Patricia Cornelius' *The Berry Man*. In August, she directed a production of her own work, *Disclosed (a performance in three cells)*, which she wrote as part of an English Honours project in 2012. Caitlin is the convenor of the Tasmanian Writers' Centre's group for young writers, Twitch, and is currently completing her Masters of Teaching.

Disapol Savetsila (*Jun/John*) is a creative writing student at the University of Wollongong. He has written plays for The Drama Studio's Final Draft Project, as well as two Theatre Versus Everything productions. In 2013, he was a winner of the ATYP's national monologue writing competition, and Stringybark's Future Times Award. Disapol has taken part in Playwriting Australia's Lotus Salon and has been published in the Stringybark Anthology *A Tick Tock Heart*, and Melaleuca Blue's *You'll Eat Worse Than That Before You Die* anthology.

Fiona Spitzkowsky (*Accidents Happen*) is a Melbourne-based writer, who has only just developed the ability to call herself that without the support of semi-sarcastic air-quotes. Her first produced work was *Room 62791* at the Canberra Youth Theatre in 2009. Since then she has completed a Bachelor of Communications (Theatre/Media), graduating with distinction. During her time at university Fiona penned scripts for the Central West Short Playwriting Festival (2013) and Sprung Festival (2012, 2013), including the highly successful comic cabaret *A World Without Sex*, which toured to Sydney and Brisbane. She was also a finalist in ATYP's Fresh Ink Competition in 2013 with *Paris*. She is currently completing a Masters in Creative Writing, Publishing and Editing at the University of Melbourne, paying the bills as the Digital Editor for Big Stories, an online documentary project, and maintaining her passion for theatre through her work with Attic Erratic and fledgling theatre company We Happy Few.

Amanda Yeo (*Pink Hair*) is a BA Communication/B Laws graduate, a SWEATSHOP: Western Sydney Literacy Movement writer, and a pop culture enthusiast. Her first play won its Wildcard division at Short+Sweet when she was 16. Since then she has performed her work at the 2012 Sydney Writer's Festival event Moving People, Bankstown's 2011 Youth Week event Own It!, and on FBI Radio's 'All the Best' segment. She has been published in the *UTS Writers' Anthology 2011: The Life You Chose and that Chose You*, *Westside New Series Vol 2: On Western Sydney*, and *Stories of Sydney*, and has spoken at the launch of the Australia Council for the Arts' Disability Action Plan for 2014-16. She attended the National Studio in 2012 and her monologue 'Red Panda' was performed as part of ATYP's Fresh Ink Out of Place showcase.

MENTOR BIOGRAPHIES

Jane Bodie is a playwright, screenwriter, mentor and director.

Jane's plays include *Music* (Griffin 2014), *This Years Ashes* (Griffin 2011), *Hallelujah* (Theatre 503 UK), *Out Of Me* (Soho Theatre UK), *Ride* (Belvoir Company B, 59E59 New York), *A Single Act* (winner of The Victorian Premiers Literary Award 2007 – Melbourne Theatre Company/Hampstead Theatre UK), and *Still, Hilt* and *Fourplay* (Trades Hall, TRS and Edinburgh Fringe). Jane was short-listed for The Ewa Czajor Memorial Award as a director and nominated for the Patrick White Playwrights' Award. She won a Green Room Award for Outstanding Writing in 2003 for *Still*.

Jane worked at the Royal Court Theatre with the Young Writers Programme and on attachment at The National Theatre UK in 2005. Jane has written extensively for TV and radio, including *The Secret Life of Us*, *Crash/Burn* and *Moving Wallpaper*. She's currently adapting *This Years Ashes* for the screen for Screen Australia.

Jane was Head of Playwriting at NIDA from 2010 –2012, Associate Artist at The Griffin Theatre in 2013 and was Artistic Associate at Playwriting Australia in 2014.

Jane Fitzgerald is a freelance Sydney dramaturg.

Her most recent project was *M.Rock* by Lachlan Philpott, co-produced by ATYP and Sydney Theatre Company (STC). She works as a Mentor with Year 12 students on HSC creative writing and has been a Mentor for ATYP's Fresh Ink.

For STC she has worked as Literary Manager, Artistic Associate and administrator of the Patrick White Playwrights' Award as well as a dramaturg on the Blueprints new writers' program and on mainstage productions.

She has worked as a script reader for the Royal Court London, Australian National Playwright's Centre, Playworks and STC Young Playwrights' Award. She has a Master of Arts in Theatre Studies from UNSW. Jane loves working with writers and is excited to be part of this year's National Studio.

Ross Mueller is an Australian playwright. He has been writing for theatre, radio and film for almost twenty years. He is the Winner of the New York New Dramatists Playwright exchange for his play *Concussion*. In March 2009 *Concussion* premiered at STC. In April 2009 his play *Hard Core* was shortlisted for the Patrick White Award. He is the winner of the Wal Cherry Play of the year 2007 for his play *The Glory*. In March 2007 his play *The Ghost Writer* premiered at Melbourne Theatre Company. *Construction of the Human Heart* was short listed for the 2007 AWGIE Award for Best New Play and nominated for five Green Room Awards. In 2002 he was the Australian playwright at the International Residency of the Royal Court Theatre in London. His most recent play *ZEBRA!* premiered at STC in March 2011.

He is currently under commission to ATYP working on a new play about the First World War entitled *A Town Named War Boy*.

ABOUT ATYP

Staff

Artistic Director
Fraser Corfield
General Manager
Aaron Beach
Finance Manager
Kate di Mattina
Development Manager
Andrew Deane
Marketing Manager
Amy Maiden
Workshop Manager
Sarah Parsons
Education Manager
Adèle Jeffreys
Production Manager
Juz McGuire
Education Co-ordinator
Lisa Mumford
Writing Co-ordinator
Jennifer Medway
Administration Co-ordinator
Elise Barton
Marketing Co-ordinator
Samantha Cable
Geek-in-Residence
Dan Andrews
Archivist
Judith Seeff
Publicist
Kar Chalmers

Board of Directors

Michael Ihlein (Chair)
Fraser Corfield
Nancy Fox
Alexandra Holcomb
Janine Lapworth
Cathy Robinson
Edward Simpson
Simon Webb
Natasa Zunic

Writers Under Commission

Patricia Cornellius (VIC)
Suzie Miller (NSW)
Tom Mesker (NSW)
Ross Mueller (Vic)
Kate Mulvany (NSW)
Sarah West (SA)

The Atypical Youth Advisors

Andrew Brophy
Emma Campbell
Airlie Dodds
Matt Friedman
Naomi Hastings
Ava Karuso
Stephanie King
Julia McNamara
Paul Musumeci
Sydney Nicholas
Kathleen Quere
Julia Rorke
Cole Scott-Curwood
Charlotte Tilelli

Cooper Torrens
Rachel Weiner
Emily Bailey Hughes
Emily Sheehan
Rebecca Cuttance
Sean Marshall

Tutors
Marika Aubrey
Josh Barnes
Guillaume Barriere
Vanessa Bates
Sarah Berrell
Anya Beyersdorf
Kylie Bonaccorso
Justin Buchta
Kathy Burns
Mitchelle Butel
Laura Buxton
Heather Campbell
Travis Cardona
Rachael Coopes
Melinda Dransfield
Curtis Fernandez
Martha Goddard
Tanya Golberg
Lyndelle Green
Sam Haft
Suzie Hardgrave
Honora Jenkins
Shane Jones
Sophie Kelly
Luke Kerridge
Amy Kersey
Natalia Ladyko
Caleb Lewis
Katie Mckee
Natasha McNamara

Jennifer Monk
Danielle O'Keefe
Conrad Page
Kirk Page
Lachlan Philpott
Paige Rattray
Natalie Richards
Sara Ritchie
Aaron Scully
Georgia Symes
Chris Tomkinson
Laura Turner
Jo Turner
Kate Walder
Janine Watson
Scott Witt
Marni Wood

BE INSPIRED.

Interact with ATYP Learning. Talk to our friendly team of Education Experts. Visit The Wharf. Join our National Classrooms. Create something unique. The possibilities are limitless.

ATYP Learning connects schools with leading industry professionals and encourages your young people to GET INVOLVED. Whether your interest is in playwriting, directing, acting, technical production or promotion, ATYP Learning has something to get you started and keep you inspired.

Our productions, workshops, online programs and resources give you the chance to interact with all aspects of theatre. Join the ATYP community on-line or in person. We specialise in creating experiences to meet the needs of teachers and students. All of our programs are connected to State and National Curricula.

1. ATYP PRODUCTIONS: ATYP productions are driven by young characters and performed by our young performers. ATYP Learning experiences includes exclusive behind the scenes experiences, support material, online classroom resources and interactive post show Q&A sessions. Live outside of NSW and can't make it to The Wharf? Join our National Classrooms and watch one of our Live Streamed Performances!

2. MONOLOGUES NOW: Want to kick start your students' IP's? We'll come to you with a special monologue experience. One of our actors from The Voices Project will come to your classroom with our expert Learning Team. Your students will get a unique monologue performance and an opportunity to analyse and unpack the process of developing and performing this important dramatic form.

3. COMMISSION A PLAYWRIGHT: ATYP specialises in commissioning new work for young Australians. Work with us, and one of our professional playwrights, to create the perfect script for your students.

4.　　MY ATYP: ATYP's Artist in Residence programs allow your entire school to become part of the ATYP family. One of our artists visits your school for regular workshops that build drama knowledge, integrates learning and leads to a performance. Use one of our specially commissioned plays or work with ATYP and one of our professional playwrights to create the perfect script for your students. We specialise in working with you to develop a program that meets the needs of your students.

5.　　ATYP WORKSHOPS: Visit us at The Wharf. We can come to you. Our workshops are developed as 2 hour sessions or full day intensives. We can tailor-make the experience to suit the needs of you and your students. All workshops cater to the needs and skill level of your students and are related to State and National Curricula. We offer workshops for junior and senior students.

Visit our website for full workshop descriptions and booking forms atyp.com.au/education/secondary-workshops

See a production, do a workshop. Engage with us for a term, make a date with us annually, connect the dots with a tailor-made experience. We can come to your school or community!

ATYP Learning is not one-size-fits-all. We inspire you to interact with our industry professionals in a way that suits you.

The possibilities are limitless!

ACT NOW Contact our friendly learning team to book your ATYP experience Phone 02 9270 2400 Email education@atyp.com.au